A Dart of Green & Blue

Previous poetry collections by the author:

Walking on Tiptoe (Staple First Editions, 1998)
The Bat Detector (Wrecking Ball Press, 2005)
Walking on Tiptoe & Other Poems (Bluechrome Press, 2007)

A Dart of Green & Blue
Elizabeth Barrett

PUBLICATIONS
2010

Published by Arc Publications
Nanholme Mill, Shaw Wood Road
Todmorden OL14 6DA, UK
www.arcpublications.co.uk

Copyright © Elizabeth Barrett 2010
Design by Tony Ward
Printed by MPG Biddles Ltd
King's Lynn, UK

978 1906570 65 1 pbk
978 1906570 66 8 hbk

ACKNOWLEDGEMENTS:
Some of the poems in this collection, or earlier versions
of them, first appeared in *Magma, Poetry Review, Poetry
Salzburg Review, Other Poetry, The Rialto, Scintilla* and *The
Shop*. 'Kingfisher' won a prize in the Nottingham Poetry
Competition 2006 and appeared in a competition
anthology.
    A number of people have supported the writing of
this book in various ways. The author would like to
acknowledge Sheffield Hallam University who provided
her with some time to write and members of her women's
writing group for helpful feedback on early versions of
the poems. Pete Lyons transcribed Blackbird's song (p.
47) and helped with the grace notes. Matthew Clegg has
been a loyal and candid critic, and Caroline Bath and
Karen Dunn have offered their unfailing support. Some
of the poems in this collection emerged from *The Healing
Touch*, a collaboration with the artist John Brokenshire;
the author gratefully acknowledges his influence on her
palette. The author would particularly like to thank
Catcher for inspiration and support, and for the light at
the end of this book.

Cover: "Floating Free Thirty Three"
by John Brokenshire, © 2010

Supported by
**ARTS COUNCIL
ENGLAND**

Editor for the UK and Ireland: John W. Clarke

*In memory of
my mother, Barbara,
1934-2006*

Contents

– Even losing you (the joking voice, a gesture
I love) I shan't have lied. It's evident
the art of losing's not too hard to master
though it may look like (*Write* it!) a disaster.

Elizabeth Bishop, 'One Art'

I
KINGFISHER

Equinox

This Spring I'll tip the scales to *day* –
tilt them with weighted hours, then fold
time here at the edge of light. I will stay
with her at the high window, gold
flaring long as a solstice sun. We'll play
at naming streets and she'll admire the bold
yellow flower on the Arts Tower. From her bay
window on Ward Q3 (Acute) I'll hold
back the night, so she'll never look the way
she did next day when she'd been told.
There will be no fall through shortened days,
no sudden winding down of years, no scald
of tears nor darkness. Blessed in gold,
the day unbalancing forever, she'll grow old.

Kingfisher

In those last days she objected (gently)
to the trays of drugs the nurses brought:
I'm not a kingfisher she told me.
Swallowing was hard. She hadn't caught
those pills in river light – didn't have the king
bird's knack of flicking them in the air
until they perfect-angled down the o-ring
of her open throat. Her daily catch was square-
or zeppelin-shaped. She had to get
the pitch just right so they would slip
like silver fish into her failing gullet –
otherwise she'd gag on them, be sick.
On her last day they pumped morphine through
her veins. I waited. Watched. It only took one
hour before a dart of brilliant green and blue
flashed past me (heading somewhere) and was gone.

May

Everything slow this year. Heavy and green with rain
hawthorn hung stubborn, withholding the May.
At the edge of my distracted sight I may
have caught the vaguest sign of change the day
she died. But it was the next day
(the 4th) I woke to an absence of rain.
Cruel – indifferent – the sun rose again
and, as if spring was remembering itself again,
buds opened. Even the wisteria she'd said may
not flower threw clusters of blue jewels. All day
I thought: *She's missed it. It's too late.* Last May
we walked the hedgerows on the Edge. The rain
had drawn the hawthorn's musky scent that day:
brings death, I'd thought, as I broke a branch of May.

Liminal

Friday afternoon. Two days after. My daughter
already on *Runescape*, Dylan haunting the fridge
just back from school. A friend there too,
keeping an eye. I'm upstairs, sorting things out,
when a sing-song greeting flies into the house:
Hello Dylan. It's her familiar intonation;
the joyous voice she keeps for him.
I hesitate. Peer downstairs.
My speechless son is opening cupboards
in self-absorbed silence. His sister
(eyes fixed to the screen) apologises:
no, sorry – she hasn't said hello to him.
It was Sunday before the friend said:
I thought I heard your mum the other day.

Matriarch

Was she still with us two days before
the funeral I had not planned? The only time
I went back to her house. I asked her other daughter
why I'd been left out. She gave it to me straight:
Because you're an arse. I asked for more.
I don't talk to people I don't like my sister said.
Something in the pull of her mouth, the way
the right side reared itself, convinced me.
I cursed her and turned my back. Then, from behind,
my mother's husband kicked me down the steps.
How finely she held the balance: the stepfather
I couldn't forgive; a resentment of siblings.
And how quickly it all unravelled; all of us,
pulling at threads, unpicking her stitches.

Lights, Bangs, Flashes

All the next week, bangs and flashes of light bulbs
extinguishing themselves. There was no pining,
no high-pitched whine to warn me they were near the end;
just a series of sudden deaths. One morning, the force
of four at once threw the screen in the cooker hood
from its seating. Everything kept fusing in my newly-
wired house. How many trips did I make to the cellar,
fumbling through the floor hatch in torchlight to trip
the circuits back? One night, bulbs jumped clean from
their bayonets, flung out of their screwed-down lives.
Was this her doing; a code for me to crack?
What was she trying to signal through this black-out
and flash? I wasn't sure until the day, stopped at lights,
a car slammed me from behind. The impact threw
me from my seat, knocked both his headlamps out.
I hugged him, kissed his cheek. *I'm so sorry,* I said.

Mother

From Dylan's bridge, where a waterfall disrupts the brook,
I saw her standing on a rock, neck outstretched. Her ducklings were adrift – the sord split – and the mother duck
was balanced between those above the falls and three stuck
at the foot. I watched as one of the ducklings stuck
to turning hopeless circles downstream in the brook.
The other two were trying to jump back up. *Dylan, look!*
I urged as one was hurled back by the water. By luck
it surfaced in a crevice of the rock and scrambled clear. The duck
behind played follow my leader. Two up. For the one still stuck
things didn't look so good; the left-behind scrap of duck
was fading, drifting from side to side further down the brook.
What would a mother do I wondered? Save the one still stuck
and risk the others? Or cut her losses – sacrifice the lone duck?

Lambs

At Whitsuntide I walk once more up to the Edge.
The promised day has turned to rage; I fight
for every step, cling to dry stone wall and hedge.
The rain cascades in grey; mother-of-pearl light
tips out of the sky. I find a curled-up lamb
and think it dead, but as I pass its thin bleat
catches the wind. As a child I'd call her name
when I woke dizzy and alone; I'd stumble to my feet
crying *mum*. And suddenly, at my side, a lone ewe
zigzags across the Edge, pausing then calling –
her head poised in the air, listening. What could I do
but leave her searching? On the way down, in falling
rain, I listened for her lamb. Nothing. Death
had come swiftly it seemed. But as I stared
a new lamb emerged. There were two. The ewe's grief
was doubled then – and the loss of her, shared.

Losing Things

Midsummer. The longest day draws out the crowds –
families, couples, girls downtown. I watch their eyes
for tell-tale signs but pick up only smiles; it will last
forever they think. Don't they know how fragile
this is? And once you've lost the toughest things –
daughter, mother – why bother holding on to others?
So I quit the job I'd just got; didn't care for the boss.
Told a woman I'd never trusted where to get off.
My mum had *her* number. She was smart enough
not to judge my lover. Still, I chucked him too.
The house went on the market next. One week I peeled off
three people (cross me you're dead). Others I quietly dropped.
Soon there was nothing else to lose. I was travelling light
through voodoo June turning day to night, sun to moon.

Equinox

I want to lose my balance; go somewhere uncertain,
beyond reason. The clairvoyant names the date and hour
of death. *Do you know she loves lilies? Always think of her*
with flowers. She tells me you were never good at picking
men. She let you make your mistakes. For some reason
she puts fish around you. Please remember I told you.
She pins a brooch on you, shows me one white rose.
Your mum loves Christmas. She was a good cook.
She doesn't want you to be sad this year, my love.
But she would like you to be more consistent.
She makes me aware of letters being burned.
She's not happy about it. No, she's not happy at all.
Do you understand? The spirit world has many ways
of making things happen. She wants you to leave it alone.
And you'll be connected to an Irish man, I'll say that.
I buy lilies – book a week in County Kerry for luck.

Solstice

I count the shortening days to Solstice Eve –
stand each advent afternoon in winter light.
A slant of sun casts this room into relief –
long shadows repossess the last white
breath of light. My simple Christmas wreath
greets the longest night. I ache for her bright
voice to praise my plaited ring of ivy leaves,
to ask (so we avoid repeats) what she might
give her grandchildren this year. I do believe
she's gone – I wish there were some respite
from belief in loss. But even in the night
my clocks don't stop; absence takes light
hold and keeps a steady watch. There's no relief.
Night outruns the sun and days dissolve to grief.

Hem

Afterwards, my daughter always wore
the pyjamas my mother made her.
It comforted her – the idea her Gran
was with her through the night,
touching her. Sometimes, though,
I found her crying, this last gift
too dear, too hurtful now, to bear.
One night, standing ready for bed,
there was no avoiding it: the legs
had risen half way to her knees.
We were still unhealed; nothing
to be done but sit in a circle of light
snipping at thread – unpicking her last
stitches, unfolding my mother's hem.

II
GULL VIEW NORTH

I

Isle of Slingers, lands of the King, white tablet
　　　licked by salt, dipping and tilting gently
　　　south in wrinkles of light from the east.
　　　Carved by time from a single stone – no one
　　　between stone and the Crown Court of sea
　　　and sky. Ack-ack. Ack-ack. The gulls
　　　squabble, hold the high air's Leet.

II

Pulpit Rock. Hallelujah. Dead Man's Bay. Sea-struck
　　　land with one bound stone on a shingle bank.
　　　Waves heave themselves onto the beach
　　　and pull back. She can hardly stand – picks
　　　her way through pebble heaps dragging at her feet.
　　　Above the clatter disturbed stones whisper:
　　　here is the way to slowly end, to disappear.

III

Beneath her feet the Island beats a rhythm of salt flats
        and lagoons. This is where the best beds
        of stone lay down – here, where dinosaurs
        walked and the overburden is excessive.
        One hundred and forty five million years.
        Soil, Slate, Shivered Stone, Clay.
        Aish, Soft Burr, Dirt Bed, Skull.

IV

She turns a bird's eye, rises with the skylarks over it;
        the island dips in a south-south westerly wind,
        a tethered moon lifting its bleached face to the sky.
        In Dead Man's Bay the wind drives lerrets onto cliffs.
        At the Island's tip a man sits staring out to sea,
        caught in silver light. His back has set to stone.
        He is counting fish: Mullet, Mackerel, Sea Bass.

V

Lines of weakness. Gullies running through the whole
      sequence. Vertical fractures where the land slid,
      toppled north-north east to south-south west,
      up-dip. She leaps them like a long ear, joints
      crossing at right angles beneath her outstretched
      feet. This is where pig places are cut, wedges
      driven in; the surface turned higgledy-piggledy.

VI

Wedding. Jump three times over the iron rod; that one
      used for drilling. Wear a hat. Stand up straight.
      Sing *The French Song*. Sink plugs and feathers.
      Drive the wedges in. Ream up! Ream up!
      Pig place. Pig face. Her cheeks are grooves
      of cuneiform. The clouds have blown to stone.
      The whitecaps carve themselves upon the sea.

VII

When he takes her nipple between his teeth
        a voice echoes on the white stone walls.
        She does not believe in even the gulls.
        If she were to shoot one it would shatter,
        fall to earth as pieces of clay. Deep, deep
        in the bed the kimmeridge lies. His feet
        grow heavy. She turns her implacable face.

VIII

This is how men enter: by drawbridge and door
        into a tunnel which leads to stone
        through a labyrinth of rooms they have hewn
        from rock. This is the citadel where they are kept.
        She wants to walk the circumference, to know
        the wire and Panopticon caves. She wants to reach
        the warning light, to assess her chances of escape.

IX

Eight hundred thousand men have earned this honour
        – the best bed – by gunshot and bayonet. Won
        their stones by skewering of limbs, loss of eye.
        Stone of the dead. Whispering stone.
        Stone of banquets and feasts.
        Bring the King's mutton; those hardy ewes
        with close wool are sure-footed. Slaughter the beasts!

X

The stones are sleeping. They have nothing mortal
        about them. But they long to be redeemed:
        to be touched by her passing, to be received
        as gift. The stones are incantations.
        They have captured and imprisoned one thousand
        souls. The stones are dreaming of movement
        and gesture; judgement beautiful as a dream of stone.

XI

Oolith, oolith, oolith. Basebed, Whitbed, Roach.
      Creamy fish roe. Horse's Heads. Pure white
      fragments of fine ground shell. Forest fossils
      ghosting the stone. Under the kivel she sees
      an angel. Tap tap. Dust on her hands, in her face.
      Close your eyes! Quick! There are diamonds
      and necromancers glinting in the cracks.

XII

In Suck Thumb Quarry the flowers are flying;
      powder blue petals in the air. Silver studded
      blues. Trefoil. Eyebright. There are winning
      chains around the bleached blockstone.
      It is sweetly stacked. Scooped walls sink
      to an apron of white, the bottom of the world
      sublime. On the north wind she hears bells ringing.

XIII

The sea sucks at soft cliffs, eating through white
       tablets and stacks; it turns the stone to crumble,
       breaks through the land. Her footprints
       leave chalkdust tracks. The rain
       and sea will come. If she looks back,
       over her shoulder, she could turn to stone,
       let him go. Overhead the white gulls drift.

XIV

Gull truth is three-sided: East, South, West.
       Mullett, Mackerel, Sea Bass. Gull view
       north is pebble-bank; a strand of scavenged
       land. Gull considers speck of girl face down,
       arms outsplayed, by the bound stone.
       Gullshit place. In a wing's beat, by a stretch
       of shadow, she is erased; full gull eclipse.

III
PENELOPE'S MAGPIE

Forest

This is where they enter – by a track
of orange needles, the ground yielding
beneath their feet. At either side,
purple stumps of cut spruce one foot high.
Aren't the dead trees wonderful, he says.

And of course (this is a magic poem)
they stray from the path; pass a pile
of fallen branches forwards and back,
stumble twice across a dry stone wall.
Is the light darker here? she asks.

When they emerge by a different path
they are holding hands. If they were six
you'd think them sister and brother.
Their auburn heads brush against each other
as they slink like fox cubs past the reservoir.

*

That night, when she undresses, she finds
muddy prints across her right breast, a sticky
smear of feathers on her belly – she plucks
orange needles from between her thighs,
discovers bright hair growing above her wrists.

Storm

The photos he was taking
took flight when they stopped talking.
She settled her gaze on his slim hands,
the shape of them around his camera
framing a golden aperture.

She tried to fly between the gates of his hands
into his lens; to aim herself feather and bone
at him. She imagined she could free fall
and he would catch her – hold her
up in the hollow of his palm.

As they downloaded the photos she was caught
in a field of light from the left hand side,
the colours exploding – a red fox curled
in her hair and at her throat, suddenly,
hummingbird wings beating.

   *

That evening she perched in her attic room
watching flashes of light thrown
across a hunter's moon. Two blackbirds
flew upwards, suddenly, then settled
back into a neighbour's tree.

And she thought of him on the hill
above her; held, anchored by family.
On the shipping news she heard the force 10
storm would lose its identity by dawn.
She clung to her rock, waiting to sleep him off.

Penelope's Magpie

Today she is feverish in white,
her body a drift of feathers.
He settles raggedy on her sheets
in his black coat and hat –
says, in answer to her trembling
admission, that it's alright.
As she reaches across the bed,
searching for water, he bends
to peck his kisses in her back.

I want to see you grow your silver hair
he says, *for this to last.*
She lifts her gaze to his face
when he offers this unasked. Such faith
she thinks. He barely knows her –
they've only met a dozen times perhaps;
exchanged emails, photographs.
Besides, he has a life elsewhere
why would he want her silver hair?

Like a magpie wedding in winter
she tells herself as she unpicks
the glittery stitches from her crown.
She is stealing time – concealing
the silver herringbone at her temples
and roots. She weaves in red threads,
keeps her hair a foxy brown.
She will make her magpie lover wait
for a hint of silver, the first glint of winter.

Keel

He sits in the crook of her back
as she lays face down on the bed –
slides his hands under to push
her vest up past the sternum
and over her neck. Her breast
slips tenderly into his palm.
This is the plumpest place
where the flight muscles grow.
This is where clavicles fuse
to wishbones at their ends,
opening and closing again.

Here, under his hands,
she will find her deep keel;
grow an anchoring bone to hold
the wings' load. She imagines
the whirr and flap of them beating,
the muscles pulsing in her breast.
He parts the hair at the base
of her neck – checks the way
the air-filled bones at the nape flex.
This is the fusing place; they keep
their balance, hold their strength.

Keel: a ridge along the breastbone of many birds.

Seven Magpies in a School Car Park

The first is Sorrow
though she doesn't know she has
reason to be sad.

Joy swoops in. She shines
darkly in love's feathers, bright
button eyes darting.

Three is for the Girl
Joy has flown without warning
to collect today.

Raggedy Boybird
is next on the scene, here to
meet his magpie wife.

He is shocked to see
Sorrow and Joy side-by-side –
Silver at the crown

of Joy, a Gold ring
around unknowing Sorrow.
Magpie Boy stays cool,

unruffled. He gives
nothing away as Joy flaps
her wings anxiously.

Thoreau's Mouse

he tells her, would visit
the simple hut by that pond –
take cheese from clean between
Thoreau's fingers.
Imagine, he says, *such trust*.

As they skirt a stand of sycamores
he falls suddenly to the ground,
drops like a kestrel. He claws
at the wet brown mulch
raking leaves through his hands.

Every woman I've loved,
he says, *it ends this way.*
She stays perfectly still – lets herself
imagine she could simply reach
between his fingers, take the leaf.

Snow Dreaming

As they entered the beech wood
she looked across at snow dreaming
on Mayfield Hill – imagined their tracks
on the untrodden slope, later, when they'd
looped back. They would have crossed
unspoken lines by then perhaps –
slipped their bounds to pass like ghosts
through kissing gates and stiles.
Their feet would be free as white birds
gliding to the end of the unweighed world.

*

Under the beech wood's winter canopy –
its branches lacing the low sun to sky –
they pause at the head of a gorge.
One of them is about to say something,
or reach out perhaps for the other,
when suddenly there is a rush of air
on their faces, ghost wings beating downriver.
She turns too late; stands unseeing, unheld
beneath the beech. But his eyes
are trembling: *Did you see that?* they quiver.

*

Is that why he spoke the words he did
as they returned by Mayfield Hill?
The grey-winged clouds blew in,
heard him unburden his fear and guilt,
stumble his way to the end of it.
And then the dread; a stillness settling
in the trees as they walked undreaming.
She imagined they might meet themselves
heading up the valley; that they could untrace
their snowy tracks, pause forever by the river.

Pelican Lent

She is learning to live
under a sky which widens without him.
She knows the clouds are not white
since he showed her herring bright,
salmon light, river brown.

Her voice turns to howl
in the valley which thickens without him.
She drifts between trees, her slashed bib
bleeding from her breast on the right.
She goes to the spruce at night –

the one with the spidery rim
round a heart-shaped hole. Perhaps he will
leave something there for her – she might
find lambs' wool. In bruised light
she lays her cheek to the ground –

listens for the steady sound
of him breathing, his body's hymn
as he mixes colours, makes them sing.
She prays this sacrifice – no sight
of him – will resurrect their flight.

*The pelican is reputed to self-wound by stabbing herself in the breast, and to kill
her young then resurrect them with her own blood.*

Bird Evolution

'Birds might continue to evolve for another billion years… but they surely will never produce great poets, or philosophers, or professors of jurisprudence'.

Colin Tudge, *Consider the Birds*

Heron is holding court:
It is wrong to take what isn't yours by river-given law
he proclaims to the birds in the beech copse.
Heron knows Magpie has been stealing.
He must give up the nest he wove from silver hair
and filled with glittery crystals.
I was only stealing a bit of happiness Magpie protests.
You must give it back, Heron replies, *and live without whiteness.*

*

Pelican knows her breast won't bleed forever –
that with time it will heal. That she'll no longer stoop
to hear him breathe; she'll lift her keening cheek from the ground.
She knows, one day, she will not feel the urge to cut;
there'll be no need for lambs' wool then to staunch her blood.
She will stop going to the spruce in the wood.
Pelican knows how love can turn to this: self-harm, self-sacrifice.
For chance of joy she takes the risk.

*

Listen. Blackbird is singing still in your neighbour's tree.
How sweetly she rhymes! Hear her voice lilt on the wind,
her soft notes scan from leaf to leaf –

47

IV
FINCH

Delta Wings

1 Flight Path

A child had died and she was living
in a wedge-shaped room of whitewashed walls
and glass close to Heathrow
on a flight path with geese and swans.
Their cries lifted leaves from trees
like the hairs at the back of her neck,
dragged furrows through the stand of water
in the disused quarry, its surface trembling
like a held-back tear's collapse.
And each afternoon at four o'clock
she'd rush to the door, drawn by the roar
of torn air – tilt her face to the swept back
shape of those delta wings, that pointy nose
the pilot had to lower and lift.

II CRASH

Tonight they are watching footage
of the crash; she holds her other daughter
in her arms as it belly flops along the track,
the wings cut-paper angels on black tarmac,
its nose scraping and sparking
along the ground. A plume of white smoke
pours from one of the engines on the port side.
Her daughter is troubled by the rubble
on the runway; that an unswept track could cause
a crash. So they talk about why it's important
to do things well, whatever the task – she says
this to the child heavy-hearted, knowing
the struggle to keep a marriage intact in a place
far from water, away from flight paths.

iii Grounded

These are the delta rhythm days;
pale waves of light dancing on still wings
sleeping in lines. She wonders whether
the ocean misses the boom of their coming –
if it is bored and empty without them.
She worries that their white paint might
peel and flake away from the engine's growl.
She tells her growing daughter how they flew
a 2.7 second mile, travelled improbably
half way round the world in record time.
That they stretched by ten inches in flight.
She cannot bear this thought – them shrinking,
now, on the ground. Her world has grown flat;
the planet's curve vanished from the window.

IV DELTA WINGS

She often spoke of it – the dream of flying.
Now her daughter is sad because it isn't true.
The mother remembers how someone
she promised died too soon – wants to tell
her daughter they are simply out of time.
But she changes her mind.
It's the night before they've vowed
to tell her; she knows it's really
her letting the daughter down.
So instead she says it isn't the flying
as much as trembling in its shadow
on the ground; to witness the grace
of those delta wings lifting to the high above –
feeling a rush of air, the urge to look up…

Say then

Say that the colour of your shirt
reflected the lake in your eyes,
that the pitch of your alto voice
made me tremble inside.

Say that you noticed the watery beads
of glass around my neck, gestured
to a seat as if you had expected this –
offered paper, steaming tea, a pen.

Say that at the sound of your name
I unwound, as if I'd known always
that in a carriage of strangers I would
reach to brush dust from your cheek.

Say that it was fear of this
made me long for the train to slide
from the tracks of that wooden bridge –
to hang suspended over the glittering lake.

Say then that I would fly
like a trapeze girl letting go of the rope,
feel water the colour of your eyes
going over me, filling my throat.

Grace Notes

The scarcely perceptible shape of your smile
as you turn to look at me on this silent tier of steps,
the winter sky glinting like crushed ice.

♪

I lean into your arm. This moment
doesn't count; it is *kan-swar*, a touch note only.
It is up to us how long we stay this way.

♪

Some days there are doublings and birls:
a trill in my nerves when I hear your name,
the coil of your voice through my telephone line
dancing the stave of roof tops and wire.

Now I improvise, play extra notes on the beat
of my heart: bless your bike through the rainy
arabesque of city streets; may you sleep like a baby
with closed fists; let me hold my face to yours *like this*.

♪

There is harmony enough in the slur of light
on your cheek, the motes of dust. But now you garland it;
lift your sweater over your head so the air shakes.

In Indian music grace notes are known as kan-swars or touch notes.

Finch

I INNER HORIZON

From across this space where you sit
in the slant of light from that window
your eyes absorb sky, reflect
the colour of weather like water.
If we stare long enough at each other
there will be a bang of agapanthus blue.
Lake-eyed man I would dive into you;
leap from this chair, fly through the air.

II EVENT HORIZON

Like Niagara: the point of no return
for the boat in a pulse of dark water
at the top of the Horseshoe Falls.
I want to reach for you but I must balance
on this wire, held by only your eyes.
If I look down I will lose the curve of space
and time – fly to you in a straight line and slam,
like a bird, against your window.

III THE SINGULARITY

Where it begins.
The flash of me and you.
It is small and heavy here.
We occupy no space at all.
We are an impossible object
at the heart of a black hole
or the beginning of time.
This is where our understanding
of nature breaks down.

IV BLACK HOLE

Open your eyes wide enough to catch
a wounded finch. Guide me in. I will
sing while I dive through your windpipe,
weave my song in your labyrinth
of tissue and bone. I will preen your lungs,
beat my broken wing against your heart.
What? You mouthe at me: *What?*
There's no sound when I try to respond.

v Curved Starlight

Someone is looking for us; we give nothing away.
This is stillness: we emit no waves of sound
or light. We are the stopped heart of a vortex,
the dark crown in a halo of curved starlight.
Does she know that if she sees nothing
she has found us? That we are plus and minus?
Outside the light is turning itself down;
a far horizon sparkles with phosphorescence.

Notes on 'Gull View North'

Some of the details in 'Gull View North' are drawn from Peter Trim *The Quarrying of Portland Stone* (1991) and Rachel Barton and Peter Revell *Portland Stone Experience* (2005).

(p. 27) I: *Isle of Slingers* is the name given to Portland by Thomas Hardy who described it as 'carved by time out of a single stone'. The Royal Manor of Portland is directly answerable to the Crown; a Court Leet, comprised of representatives of the Crown and tenants, is still in existence.

(p. 29) v: Rabbits are believed to be omens of bad luck, blamed for rock falls in quarries. A local superstition suggests that calling rabbits by their proper name brings bad luck. Pig places are grooves which were cut into the base of the block of stone; pieces of pig iron were inserted into these grooves and four wedges were then placed between each of the 'Pigs'.

(p. 29) VI: At local weddings the groom would traditionally jump three times over an iron rod, or 'jumper', used for drilling. Those present at the ceremony not standing correctly or wearing a hat would be fined and the monies given to the groom. Traditionally, 'The French Song' was sung by quarrymen to ensure unison while wedges were being struck. Plugs and Feathers are a more modern device used in splitting blocks; these are placed in a series of pre-drilled holes. 'Reaming up' describes the moment when the block is prised away from the main layer of stone.

(p. 30) VIII: Convicts were first transported to Portland in 1848. There is still a prison, HMP Verne, on the island.

(p. 31) IX: Portland stone was used in the construction of a number of significant buildings including St Paul's Cathedral, the Cenotaph and the Banqueting Hall at Westminster.

(p. 31) x: This section adapts lines by Baudelaire ("I am beautiful as a dream of stone"), Rodin (sculpture is an "incantation by which the soul is brought down into the stone") and Rilke ("There were stones asleep, and one felt that they would awake at some Judgement Day, stones which had nothing mortal about them, and others embodying a movement, a gesture, which had retained such freshness that it seemed to be preserved here only until some passing child should receive it one day as a gift.") all taken from G. Dyer *Apropos Rodin* (2006).

(p. 32) xi: Necromancers are harmless little people who live in walls. 'Nanny diamonds' are also stone dwellers, believed to give passers-by the evil eye.

Biographical Note

Born in Sheffield in 1961, Elizabeth Barrett has a first degree and PhD in History and Politics from the University of London and was a scholarship student at the University of Massachusetts in the 1980s. She later trained as an English teacher, subsequently working in education research and as a university lecturer.

Elizabeth has received several awards for her poetry including an Arts Council of England Writer's Award in 2000. She has worked as a writer-in-residence in schools, a prison and radio, and as a creative writing tutor and poetry editor. *A Dart of Green and Blue* is her fourth book.

She has two children and lives in Sheffield where she is Principal Lecturer in Education at Hallam University.

Recent titles in Arc Publications'
POETRY FROM THE UK / IRELAND include:

LIZ ALMOND
The Shut Drawer
Yelp!

JONATHAN ASSER
Outside The All Stars

DONALD ATKINSON
In Waterlight: Poems New,
Selected & Revised

JOANNA BOULTER
Twenty Four Preludes & Fugues on
Dmitri Shostakovich

JAMES BYRNE
Blood / Sugar

THOMAS A CLARK
The Path to the Sea

TONY CURTIS
What Darkness Covers
The Well in the Rain

JULIA DARLING
Sudden Collapses in Public Places
Apology for Absence

CHRIS EMERY
Radio Nostalgia

LINDA FRANCE
You are Her

KATHERINE GALLAGHER
Circus-Apprentice
Carnival Edge

CHRISSIE GITTINS
Armature

RICHARD GWYN
Sad Giraffe Café

MICHAEL HASLAM
The Music Laid Her Songs in Language

A Sinner Saved by Grace
A Cure for Woodness

MICHAEL HULSE
The Secret History

BRIAN JOHNSTONE
The Book of Belongings

JOEL LANE
Trouble in the Heartland
The Autumn Myth

HERBERT LOMAS
The Vale of Todmorden
A Casual Knack of Living
(COLLECTED POEMS)

PETE MORGAN
August Light

MICHAEL O'NEILL
Wheel

MARY O'DONNELL
The Ark Builders

IAN POPLE
An Occasional Lean-to

PAUL STUBBS
The Icon Maker

SUBHADASSI
peeled

LORNA THORPE
A Ghost in My House

MICHELENE WANDOR
Musica Transalpina
Music of the Prophets

JACKIE WILLS
Fever Tree
Commandments